My Grandmother's Hands

Sheila Sweeny
Photography by Joel Benjamin

Rigby

My grandmother's hands are soft and wrinkly. They are very strong.

My grandmother's hands
work hard.
They fix broken things
in the house.

My grandmother's hands
brush my hair every morning.
They put my hair up
in a pretty ponytail.

My grandmother's hands
are flipping the pancakes
I eat for breakfast.
They take tasty treats
out of the oven, too!

My grandmother's hands hold my hand when I cross the street.
They make me feel very safe.

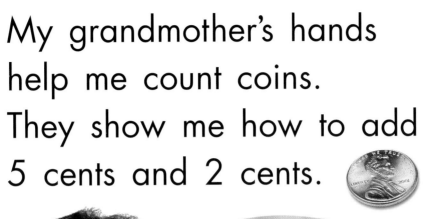

My grandmother's hands
help me count coins.
They show me how to add
5 cents and 2 cents.

My grandmother's hands clap a beat that makes me tap my toes.
They clap, clap, clap along with all my favorite songs.

My grandmother's hands catch the ball when I throw it. They always throw the ball back to me.

My grandmother's hands
cook the chicken and
celery I eat for dinner.
They cook all the good things
we eat every day.

My grandmother's hands
wash my face.
They scrub and scrub
until my face is clean.

My grandmother's hands turn the pages when I read my favorite story.
They always stop to point out pictures that make us laugh.

My grandmother's hands
tuck me into bed every night.
They help me feel
warm and cozy.

My grandmother's hands
do a lot of things.
They are very busy hands.

Best of all,
my grandmother's hands
tell me how much
she loves me.